Classic Cars

4937
This edition published 1996 by
Colour Library Direct
© 1987 CLB Publishing, Godalming, Surrey
All rights reserved
Printed and bound in Singapore
ISBN 1-85833-575-2

Classic Cars

Text by
ROGER HICKS

Colour Library Direct

1988 Porsche 959

PORSCHE

With high-performance cars, you normally have a choice: sheer performance, or reliability and comfort. Porsche is perhaps unique in offering at least one car which compromises on neither.

For sheer, raw performance it is hard to beat the fearsome 911 Turbo, and even the 'cooking' 911SC is in the front rank for fierce acceleration, uncompromising handling, and impressive top speed. But unlike some Italian machinery, where the paint pops off in the rain and fades in the sun, and the engine requires fettling once a week to keep it in tune, both cars are almost boringly reliable. Furthermore, the interior is surprisingly spacious, and although there is the beautiful whine of that flat-six engine, you are not deafened as you are in some bright-red V12s. What is more, the whole plot is surprisingly tractable; if you want to pootle down Rodeo Drive, you can do so without indulging in the bursts of heart-stopping acceleration alternated with tyre-screeching braking which are unavoidable with some of the Porsche's competitors.

And before the 911, there was the 356; a good deal slower, perhaps, but still with that happy combination of performance (in relation to its time) and reliability – though it must be admitted that the 356 could suffer from the tin-moth, and that rust has claimed a number of these cars prematurely. The 356 was rather more spartan than the 911, too, but it still looked beautiful and went beautifully.

Then again, there was the immortal flat-12 917, capable of well over 200 mph with the appropriate gearing. This was the car which turned Le Mans into a Porsche benefit: the 917s did the winning, while the 911s cleaned up on the Index of Performance and the class awards. Some Porsche 917s were road-legal, and along with the Ford GT40 these must rate as the most amazing sports cars of all time. In its ultimate form, the turbocharged 917/30 delivered over 1100 bhp...

Of course, there are other Porsches, though devotees of the cars with horizontally-opposed oil-cooled rear engines prefer to ignore them. There was the joint venture with Volkswagen, the 914, produced as a 914/6 with the Porsche engine and as a 914/4 with the Volkswagen motor. It was not a beautiful car, but it was less of a handful to drive than the 911, especially in the wet; for obvious reasons, the 914/4 is less sought-after. About 125,000 914s were made between 1969 and 1974, when production ceased. The reason for this cessation, at least in part, was the forthcoming launch of the 924.

The 924 horrified purists. The engine was in the wrong place (at the front); it was the wrong layout (in-line four); it had the wrong sort of cooling (water); and by the standards of Porsche in 1975, it was small at 2 litres, 122 ci (the biggest flat sixes were now 2.7 litres, 165 ci) and low-powered at 125 bhp. On the other hand, it was a very fine car, and it spawned the 924 Turbo (170, then 177 bhp) and the 'homologation special' 924 Carrera GT developing 210 bhp – the same as the original 1972 Carrera 911 RS. In 1981, the VW/Audi engine was replaced with a new 163 bhp Porsche-designed 2.5 litre four, and various 'go-faster' goodies were added to create the 944, but it was preceded in 1980 by the 928, basically a V8 version of the 924. Initially in 4.5 litre (374 ci) form with 240 bhp, it was offered two years later in 4.7 litre (387 ci) 300 bhp form.

Despite all this, the 911 refused to die, and the old flat six was bored out again; the biggest displacement to date has been the 3.3 litre (201 ci) Turbo. As a result, in the mid-to-late 1980s Porsche could offer both front- and rear-engined cars, and a range of engines which embraced an in-line four, a flat six, and a V8, with and without turbochargers – a very impressive line-up.

Somehow, history seems less appropriate when talking of Porsche than of other cars. As far as purists are concerned, there have only been two road cars – the 356, originally derived from the VW Beetle (which was, of course, also designed by Ferdinand Porsche), and the 911, though both have appeared in a variety of guises. The 356 ran from 1948 to 1965, and the 911 has been in continuous production since 1963. The other road cars are all listed above. The racing history is more complicated, and even includes a Formula One car, but that is a story which is much too long to tell here.

Facing page: (top left, top) an early 356 with split windscreen; (top left, centre) the first 356; (top left, bottom) the original 356 and a more recent model; (top right) the 356 cabriolet, which ceased production in 1965 in C form, and (bottom) the 911 Turbo, a direct descendant of the 2 litre, 130 horsepower 911 of 1963, but now with a 3.3-litre engine which develops 300 horsepower. Above: the Auto-Union racing car which bristled with innovative features, such as torsion bar suspension. Left: the very first 356, the first car to bear the Porsche name, was hand-made in Gmünd, Austria in 1948. Below left and below right: versions of the 356.

The red vehicle on these pages is a very desirable Porsche 356A (manufactured between 1955 and 1959) with a detachable hard-top offered by the factory to complement the Cabriolet body form. The flat-four engine looks diminutive inside the roomy engine compartment and it is the ancillaries that capture the attention – the cooling fan and intake filters for the carburettors being apparent immediately. For its era, the 356A Hardtop was remarkably spacious and airy. Green digits on black instruments were Porsche's trademark with the 356 model, but everything about the car was thoroughly functional and hard-wearing. Opening quarterlights in the front windows were an innovation for the A version. The silver vehicle is a pristine 356C model – with a non standard rearview mirror – in Coupé form. A total of 16,674 C models were produced between 1963 and 1965, bringing total production of the 356 up to the 76,000 mark in 16 years.

Bottom: a 356B hardtop restored to Concours standard by its American owner. Remaining pictures: a bright red 356 Speedster. The Speedster model was produced specially for the California market in America, though it was sold elsewhere in the world. It was primarily an open two-seater, though rather crude weather protection was available in the form of a black fabric hood. A total of 2,350 were made on the 356A chassis between 1955 and 1958 and are now prime collector's items. Facing page centre: the Speedster is shown beside a 911 Turbo, dubbed the Carrera Turbo in the States.

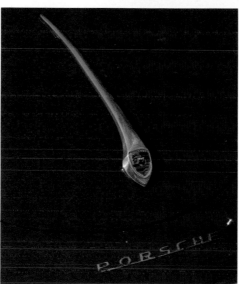

A hybrid, maybe, but a production run of 125,000 in five years spells success. The VW-Porsche 914 (this page and facing page top) was produced by a company set up jointly by Volkswagen and Porsche. The 914/4 was powered by Volkswagen's four cylinder engine and the 914/6 by Porsche's 2-litre six. Facing page bottom: a sleek example of the 911 Coupé.

Top left and top centre: the 911 Coupé. Above: a 911 Turbo. Right: a 911T, the T denoting touring trim. It was this car, which incidentally was the last normally aspirated series production Porsche (rather than having the Bosch fuel injection), which formed the basis on which the company tackled a number of sporting events with a great deal of success, notably wins in the Monte Carlo Rally in 1968, 1969 and 1970. The five-spoke, polished forged alloy wheels fitted to this car are virtually a Porsche trademark. Top right: a silky 911 Turbo. Centre right and bottom far right: two examples of the blue 911 Targa, with two different interior trims visible within the cars.

Facing page: (top left, top right and bottom right) the 3.3-litre version of the 911 Turbo which went into production in 1978; (centre) a production prototype of the 911 Turbo which had a vented grille below the rear number plate, but this did not appear in production, despite the high temperatures realised in this area by the turbocharger which spins at up to 90,000 rpm, and (bottom left) a 911. Above: a cross-section illustration of the 911, which appeared in 1963 with an air-cooled engine overslung at the rear. Left: a silver-grey 911 Turbo which first appeared with a 3 litre engine, though this was later changed to a 3.3. Below and below left: the 911 Turbo prototype.

Facing page centre: a 944. Below: a Targa. One Californian couldn't make up his mind whether he preferred black or Minerva blue, so he had both (remaining pictures). These 3.3-litre Turbos have non-standard BBS wheels and the blue car has a smart-looking customised interior. Both cars can reach the Californian speed limit of 55mph in around five seconds, but its the way you do it that really counts. Imports of the Turbo model into the USA virtually ceased in 1980 due to new emission rules coming into force, but the model remains much sought after.

Top: the powerful 944, which is based on the chassis of the 924 Carrera GT and uses the same front engine/rear transaxle layout. Above and facing page centre and bottom right: a customised 924 with BBS wheels, flared wheel arches and warm air extractors. Right and above right: a Turbo version of the 924, a model which broke entirely new ground for the company, giving it a far larger market than it had previously enjoyed. Facing page: (top left and top right) a 924 Turbo, which can deliver 177bhp from its 2-litre engine and (bottom left) a gleaming 924.

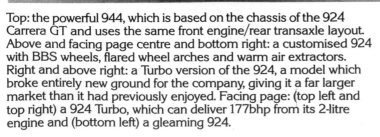

AMERICAN CLASSICS

It is perhaps in the nature of automobile lovers that most of their 'classics' are in the past. In part, of course, this is because there is far more choice if we can range over a hundred years of automobile design, rather than confining ourselves to what is available now. But some periods, in some countries, seem to breed more 'classics' than others, and most *aficionados* of American cars would claim the 1920s and 1930s as the acme of American car design: names like Cord, Duesenberg, Marmon, Packard and Pierce Arrow spring to mind.

Arguably, though, some of the greatest American classics come from after the Second World War: in a sense, there is much less to choose between the *grandes marques* on either side of the Atlantic before the war, in that they were almost all huge, impressive, weighty and powerful, and they were all designed to run on what were, by modern standards, truly appalling roads. But since the war, American and European classics have diverged so that many American classics are uniquely American. The Ford Thunderbird is an obvious example from the 1950s; the Corvette is another, first introduced as long ago as 1953; and the 'muscle cars' of the 1960s and early pre-oil-crisis 1970s, with their huge engines and shattering acceleration, surely warrant inclusion in anyone's list. Some were sports cars, more or less in the European idiom, while others such as the Buick Riviera had no equivalent on the other side of the pond: the Buick 'chairman's express' was a monster car with dramatic styling, limousine comfort, and the sheer power of a giant V8 to propel the fastest models to 60 mph in 5 seconds.

But there are other 'classics', too; it depends on how you want to define the word. For example, the All-American Finned Wonder reached its height in the 1959 season, and although the handling may have left something (or indeed everything) to be desired, for effortless cruising and spectacular looks they are hard to beat. There have also been certain *marques*, or certain models within a *marque*, that have always preserved an elegance of their own; Chrysler's styling department has had some notable successes, especially with their New Yorker line. Oldsmobile made some very impressive cars, too, and there are many names now half-forgotten, such as Desoto, Hudson and Nash. Lincolns were always serious contenders with Cadillac for the prestige market, and Cadillac themselves have their own chapter elsewhere in this book.

With few exceptions, all post-war American classics have been some way from the leading edge of automobile design. Chassis ('frame') construction lingered on long after European manufacturers had gone over to unit construction, and with plenty of cheap gasoline to sustain them, big, lazy and not particularly efficient V8 engines were the order of the day. Size alone counted for a lot, but handling (except for acceleration) and braking were rarely high on the American buyer's list of priorities. On the other hand, the 'slush-box' was standardised in the US many years ago, to the detriment of ultimate driver control but to the advantage of ease of driving.

As a result, some Europeans deny classic status to any post-war American cars, but this is a very short-sighted view: the cars were, after all, built for American and not European conditions. Wide, straight roads made few demands on handling, even in town. Huge distances meant that comfort – the celebrated 'boulevard ride' – was at a premium. Straight-line acceleration is useful for joining freeways, quite apart from its traditional fascination for Americans. A journey of four or five hundred miles, by no means an unusual day's drive makes demands on a car which are not apparent in a hundred miles or two: noise levels and spring rates which are exhilarating at first soon become tiring, and eventually downright agonising. Cruise control, first offered by Cadillac as long ago as 1959, makes long journeys very much easier. All this is a matter of experience, and usually it is a dimension of experience that European critics lack. Trying to drive a small, European-style saloon right across the United States is arguably worse than trying to drive a 1950s American behemoth in London traffic.

American classics, then, have to be accepted for what they are: American classics, not copies of European classics. It is true that on occasion the stylist's hand has been a little too heavy for European tastes, and sometimes it has been too heavy for American taste: look at the Edsel. But even then – don't you have a sneaking desire to own one?

In 1965 Ford came out with the Mustang, a sports car at a reasonable price, and it was an immediate success. In 1966, when the convertible shown here was produced, more than 600,000 vehicles were sold. The seemingly endless option list allowed customers virtually to create their own car, a feature which no doubt added to the appeal of the Mustang.

The Sedanet or Fastback styling theme had been used by Buick since 1941 and nowhere was it more attractive than on the 1949 Roadmaster Sedanet Model 76-S. The portholes on the front fenders were new, a styling gimmick that has remained a Buick trademark to this day. Note the massive over-riders on the front bumper; this was an optional feature probably designed for aggresive parking!

The breathtaking 1963 Riviera Sport Coupé was Buick's entry into the Thunderbird-dominated 'personal luxury' car market. Its razor-edged design was unlike anything else produced by GM, possessing an elegance and poise that set it apart from the rest. The Riviera was pure artistry on wheels, thanks to the gifted William L Mitchell, who blended a subtle mix of European and American influences to create a true classic.

Chevrolet produced 1,713,478 units for the 1955 model year, 773,238 of them Bel Airs (above center). The all-new styling and the first Chevrolet V8 engine since 1917 made it popular then and a collector's item today. Minor trim changes and a full width grille distinguish the 1956 model Bel Air (above top and right) from the previous year's model. Above: a 1964 Corvair Monza Spyder convertible, the last year in which this car was produced with the original body styling.

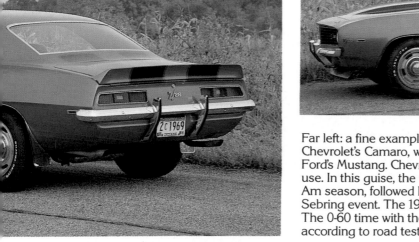

Far left: a fine example of the 1956 two-door Bel Air Sedan. Remaining pictures: Chevrolet's Camaro, which arrived on the scene a little more than two years after Ford's Mustang. Chevrolet initially dished up the impressive Z/28 option for racing use. In this guise, the Camaro beat Mustangs in the last two races of the 1967 Trans-Am season, followed by a first and second in the Trans-Am class in the 12 hour 1968 Sebring event. The 1969 Z-28 shown here has the small block 302 cid V8 engine. The 0-60 time with the 302 was slightly over 7 seconds, but the standing quarter, according to road tests, was a phenomenal 14.85 at 101.4mph.

The Billie Jo Spears song, *'57 Chevrolet* is a loving tribute to one of the best Chevrolets ever made. Its durability can be attested by its extraodinarily high survival rate, one of the many 57s still in existence is this fine example in two-toned blue and white. An option on the '57 was the famous 283 cid V8 rated at 283 hp, or one horsepower per cubic inch.

Bill Mitchell designed it, Zora Arkus Duntov engineered it and the result was the 1963 Corvette Stingray shown here. The semi boat-tail rear, novel split rear window design and pivoting, hidden headlights caused a sensation in motoring circles throughout the world. Offered as a coupé and convertible, the car was an instant success to the tune of 21,000 produced.

Chrome plate and stainless trim were in abundance on GM's 1958 models and the new Chevrolet Bel Air Impala Sport Coupé (right and next right). Remaining pictures: Briggs Cunningham's 1953 C-3 'production' model. Styled by Michelotti, then working for Vignale the Italian coachbuilders, the C-3 was one of only two American cars to be included in the New York Museum of Modern Art's list of the world's Ten Best Cars. Looking at these pictures taken on a fall evening in Florida it is easy to see why it was picked.

Not everything that came out of Detroit in the '50s was trimmed to excess. In fact the crème de la crème of Chrysler's 1955 crop, the C-300 (these pages) had extremely clean lines. This beautiful car, styled by Virgil Exner, had a New Yorker body and an Imperial grille, but the effect was striking. The C-300 was a grand tourer in every sense of the word and became the first car to hold the NASCAR, AAA and Daytona Speedworks championships at the same time.

Two years after Chrysler Corporation's 'Suddenly its 1960' look, Virgil Exner's finny styling was beginning to pall with the addition of hastily contrived trim and disorientated grilles, as in the case of this 1959 De Soto FireFlite convertible. This was unfortunate as the car had fine handling with power to match. More unfortunate was De Soto's position, sandwiched between the popular Dodge and Chrysler models. By 1961 poor sales had driven De Soto to extinction.

If ever there was a car which epitomised the flamboyant '50s, the Ford Skyliner has to be a strong contender. The retracting roof mechanism consisted of five motors, 13 switches, 10 solenoids and 610 feet of wiring. When the 'retract' switch is thrown the solid roof gracefully glides back into the over-sized trunk. Vast though the trunk was, there was barely room for a toothbrush when the roof was retracted. Only in production for three years, the Skyliner was a truly great bit of nonsense that made life worth living.

Kaiser-Frazer wasn't doing too well by 1949 and a new small car was proposed by Henry J. Kaiser to help gee things up. Shunning an attractive, small-car design from stylist Howard 'Dutch' Darrin, Kaiser settled for a concept from American Metal Products. The Henry J appeared in 1951 and sold well, but sales soon slumped and production ended in 1954.

Launched in 1961, the new Lincoln Continental (these pages) was as different from its over-ornate predecessor as chalk is from cheese. It was also unique in many ways, being the only four door convertible available anywhere with the doors opening from the center. Tooling forward of the cowl was shared with the Thunderbird to cut costs, though few could tell.

If ever there was a car which spoke for the '50s youth then it has to be the 1949-1951 Mercury. Its high waistline, rounded curves and narrow glass area begged customising and its 255.4 cid L-head V8 had enough power for cruising down the boulevard on hot summer nights. More often than not, customisers dispensed with the sliced sausage grille for something wilder and chopped the low roofline even lower. Shown here is a 1950 Mercury.

Imagine 0-60 in 6.3 seconds, a top speed of 130 mph and 9-15 miles per gallon. That's what you would have expected from a Plymouth Belvedere GTX in 1968. The GTX was one of a stable of ultra hot Chrysler musclecars, the meanest machines around, especially if equipped with the hemi 426 cid and 425 hp in stock tune. Those were the days when gasoline was plentiful and the oil companies happy for it to pour, unabated, down the gullets of a nation's increasingly thirsty cars.

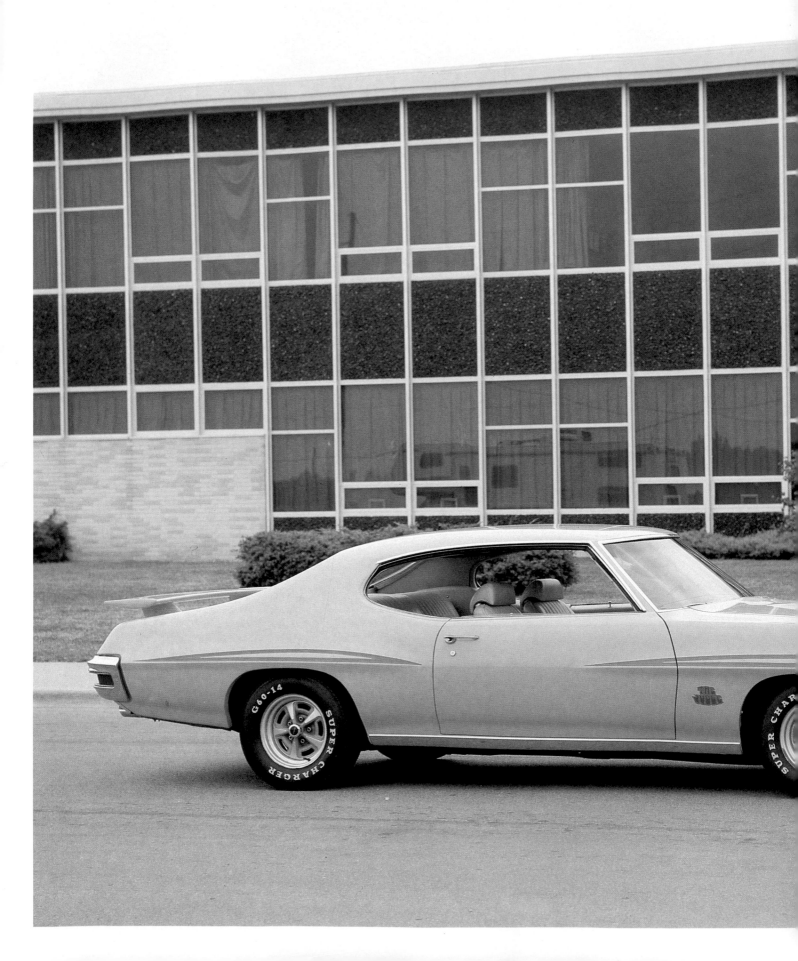

All the hoopla that went with the Judge – no doubt inspired by the Plymouth Roadrunner – disguised its true place in the musclecar scheme. It entered the fray in 1969, rather late in the day, as it happened. Not that this mattered unduly – it had, after all, the GTO's wealth of experience behind it. Never mind the dainty pink stripes, everything worked. The hood scoops, the hood-mounted tach, all were functional, while under the bonnet throbbed 400 cubic inches of Ram-Air engine which knocked up 0-60 in just over 6 seconds.

Arguably the most attractive of the three year cycle of two seater Thunderbirds was the 1957 model shown here. Slightly longer than the 1955/56 models, the last two seat T-Bird had modest tailfins flanking the lengthened trunk area. A combined front bumper/grille treatment worked commendably well. Retained from 1956 was the optional bolt-on hardtop, complete with glass portholes, which was light enought for one man operation.

Left, top and above center: the husky 1967 Pontiac GTO, one of the fastest cars of the decade. With a 400 cubic inch V8 engine the '67 GTO could reach 60 mph from rest in 4.9 seconds and complete the standing quarter in 13.09 seconds, reaching 106.5 mph. Above: the Pontiac Le Mans Sport Coupé of 1967, the family version of the GTO.

Two Studebakers, three years apart, feature on these pages. The black car is the 1953 model designed by Robert E. Bourke, chief of Loewy's Design Studio. This is a Commander State Regal Hardtop and is powered by Studebaker's 259 cid V8. The gold and white model is the 1956 Golden Hawk. It was the same body as the '53 but heavily facelifted with the inclusion of a new hood, small, classic style grille and rudimentary fins. Under the bonnet sat the big 352 cubic inch Packard engine.

Left and above: the Tucker, possibly the most advanced car of 1948, incorporated a whole host of revolutionary and advanced features, together with superb mechanics. Only 50 were produced before the project ended in the courts. Top and inset: a 1949 Jeepster, a sporty family version of the wartime jeep produced by Willys. Above center: the first Lincoln Continental, which appeared in 1940.

▲ Mercedes SL   ▼ Mercedes 260

MERCEDES

With most of the *grandes marques*, one addresses oneself to a limited range of vehicles: out-and-out sports cars, luxury cars, or perhaps sports roadsters and saloons. But Mercedes-Benz have made all of these and more, from Formula One cars to trucks, fire-engines, and ambulances. Where to begin?

One obvious place would be with the massive Benz racers from the first decade of the century, culminating in the incredible 4-cylinder 200 hp racer with a displacement of no less than 21.5 litres, 1312 ci. These chain-driven monsters were the epitome of pre-Great War racing, when brute force was all.

Another starting-point might be the S-series of supercharged straight-sixes in the 1920s and 1930s. The type numbers by which these were known are unusually informative, in that they give first the fiscal or nominal horsepower, then the actual horsepower, and finally the actual horsepower *mit Kompressor* (supercharged). Thus they began in 1927 with the 6.8 litre (415 ci) 26/120/180, otherwise known as the Sport, which delivered 120 hp unblown and 180 hp blown – the supercharger was not engaged constantly, but was only used for maximum acceleration or speed. They then progressed to a 7.1 litre (433 ci) 27/140/200 Super Sport (SS), after which they shortened the chassis by a foot and a half (50 cm) and upped the power to 27/170/225 to get the Super Sport Kurz (SSK; 'kurz' = short). Not content with that, they lightened the whole thing, race-modified the engine, and produced the 27/170/300 Super Sport Kurz Leicht (SSKL; 'leicht' = light).

After the S-series came the K-series, also supercharged, but this time straight-eights instead of sixes. By this time, they had dropped the fiscal horsepower figures, and just quoted them with and without blower. The 1934 500K was a 5-litre (305 ci) delivering 100/160 bhp, and the 1936 540K was predictably a 5.4 litre (329 ci) and delivered 115/180 bhp. But unlike, say Rolls-Royce, Mercedes also supercharged their luxury cars; the straight-eight 'Grosser Mercedes' models boasted 7.7 litres (469 ci) and a power rating which rose from 30/150/200 in 1930 to 155/230 in 1938. Rolls-Royces were quiet; (British) Daimlers were quieter; and the sound of a 7.7 litre Mercedes when the *Kompressor* cut in has been likened to the sound of a pig being slaughtered under a railway bridge.

Or again: in 1954 there was the famous Mercedes 300SL, with a 3-litre straight six in the original roadgoing 'Gull Wing'. The 300SLR racing derivative had a 3-litre straight-eight derived from the Grand Prix engines, and a top speed in excess of 150 mph with the right final drive – though the SSKL had been clocked at 156 mph nearly a quarter of a century earlier!

And yet, alongside all this ultra-dramatic machinery, there was a steady diet of mundane four-cylinder saloons. One was the Ferdinand Porsche-designed rear-engined 1300cc (79 ci) 130 H of 1933, delivering a resounding 26 hp (gross), which is remarkable chiefly for the way in which it foreshadowed the Volkswagen and (it is said) for its downright terrifying handling. Another, and perhaps the best-known, was the extremely worthy and well-made 170 series of 1700cc (104 ci) front-engined cars, made from 1935 until well after the war.

Since the war, their bread and butter models have been climbing steadily up-market, however; although the original 180 of 1953 was a side-valve in-line four, they introduced the 300-series of 3-litre (183 ci) straight-sixes in 1951, and they have steadily been extracting more and more power from them, despite reducing the actual displacement in many cases. They returned their more expensive road-going cars to the 8-cylinder fold in the 1960s, this time with a V8 rather than a straight-eight; their earlier post-war *Grosser* models used the six, while later ones used the V8, which has also found its way into many other models, including the 'Q-car' 300EL V8 6.3. Since 1955 they have also made a line of very attractive small sports cars, beginning with the pretty but not terribly fast 190SL and now including some remarkably quick V8s.

Even now, a Mercedes-Benz cannot really be compared with a Rolls-Royce. Even the most expensive models are disappointingly spartan in their basic trim, though many extras are available to make them comparable in every way with (say) a Jaguar, probably one of their nearest competitors. Where they do score is on engineering excellence; when you drive a Mercedes-Benz, you have the feeling that everything, from the engine and transmission to the door-locks, from the unitary body to the instrument fascia, has been designed and built *properly*.

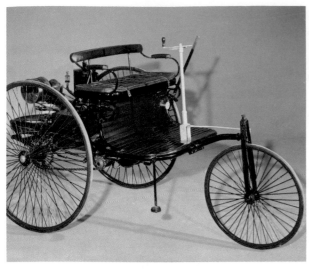

Above: the 1886 Benz three-wheeler, generally considered the world's first practical motor vehicle. Right: the wooden-framed motorcycle of 1885, which was Daimler's first vehicle. Below: the Benz 'Mylord' Coupé of 1896-99 which could reach 40 km/h. Facing page: (top) a magnificent 1908 Mercedes Edwardian tourer, with gleaming brass fittings and a dog mascot on the radiator, and (bottom) a Mercedes Simplex of 1903 with a large, limousine body.

Facing page: (top left) Daimler's first car of 1886, a converted horse-carriage; (center left) a huge 1910 limousine; (top right) the 170V of 1935; (center right) the all-conquering 1914 Grand Prix car, whose 4.5 litre engine developed 115 horsepower and won the French Grand Prix in front of a highly partisan crowd, and (bottom) the 1928 Nurnburg 460 model. Top: the 24/100/140 sportscar which had a six-cylinder, 6.2 litre engine. Above: the 320 model of 1937. Left: a short wheel-base Benz Spyder of 1902 which, although sporty in appearance, was powered by a small, 15 horsepower engine.

Facing page: (top) a Mannheim 75 horsepower car of 1931 with a solid, heavy-lined German type hood and (bottom) the 540K of 1936, which was the final statement of the supercharged sporting car. Above and overleaf: the ultimate vintage road-going Mercedes was the 1929, six-cylinder, seven litre supercharged 38/250SSK. Above right: the Targa Florio 28/95 of 1924 was also a seven litre, six-cylinder, but without supercharger. Right: the fine 1936 Sedanca Drophead 500K with coachwork by Corsica. Although somewhat dull by comparison, the 1937 saloon type 320 (below left and below right) has solid, elegant lines.

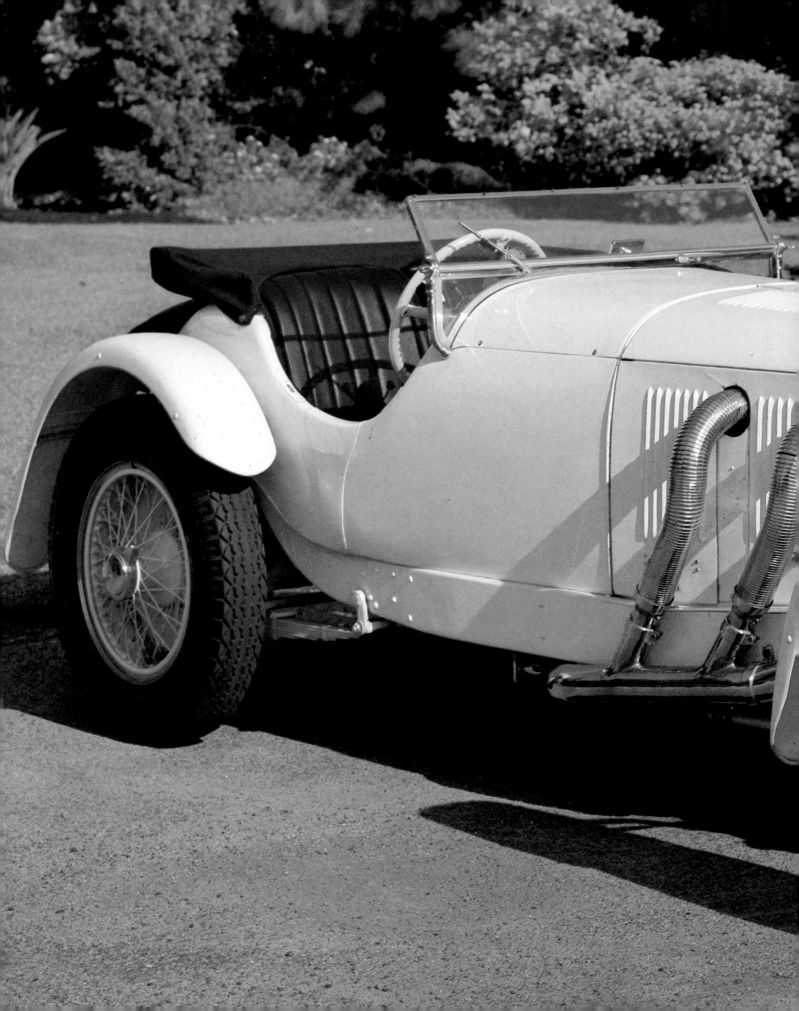

The 300SL is a rare and historic model that was made both as a conventional convertible and as a hard-top with the distinctive gull-wing doors. The open sports version is the rarer. Developed from the racing version of 1952, these 1954 cars were powered by a six-cylinder three litre engine producing 215 bhp at 5,800 rpm, with a top speed of 260 km/h. The 300SLR racing version had an eight-cylinder engine that produced 310 bhp at 7,500 rpm. Whereas the early racers used carburettors, all the road-going cars were fuel-injected.

Above: the cockpit of the 350SL (above right) which shows the high standard of finish to be found in the modern Mercedes sports car, where comfort is considered as important as performance. The 3.5 litre engine delivers 195 horsepower at 5,500 rpm. Top left: the latest S series, shown here in coupé form, is possibly the most elegant to date. Right: the much acclaimed 450SEL Bottom far right: a 1955 300SL in open roadster form. Centre far right: three fine examples of Mercedes sporting machines, from left to right the models are 280SL, 380SL: and a 500SL Top far right: reminiscent of the Grosser Mercedes of pre-war years, this picture shows the luxurious 600, with hood to the rear passenger section.

Right: the sleek sophistication of a 250C. Below: a 1968, 6.3 litre 300 SEL. Facing page: (top) the modern 380SEL; (centre left) wind tunnel tests are carried out on prototype models to determine the most efficient shape; (bottom left) stylists work on scale models of possible new designs as well as a full-sized version in the background; (centre right) the factory at Gaggenau and (bottom right) the 300SEL, introduced in 1969. Overleaf: the Daimler-Benz motor museum: (inset top left) a 500K supercharged roadster; (inset bottom left) an SSK; (inset top right) a 1934-36 type 500K special roadster and (bottom right) a 1936-39 supercharged 540K.

1936 - 39   Mercedes-Benz „540 K" mit Kompressor

H 3000

Right: a 280SE 3.5 litre convertible with its now somewhat dated lines. Below and below right: made between 1956 and 1959, the 220S had a 2195 cc, six-cylinder engine developing 100 horsepower at 4,800 rpm. Bottom: the classic 300SL shown against the much later SL model featuring the four headlamp arrangement. Facing page: (top, centre left and centre right) the 300S was faster than the invincible pre-war supercharged seven-litre models. It had an engine half the size of its predecessor, but was one ton lighter and, except for the fuel injected SC model, it used three carburettors. Bottom right: a 1968 300SEL.

Above: a 280SL. Below centre left: a comparison of aerodynamics. Remaining pictures: the 170S cabriolet, which developed from the saloon model. The 170 was made in 1935 and again in almost indistinguishable form in 1949-52. The standard post-war models were the saloon, convertible and convertible saloon or cabriolet.

Top: as with many modern sporting models, the bonnet-top badge of the SEC is absent. Above: the sleek good looks of the 500SLC. Right: the 280S. Far right: the 480SE, powered by an eight-cylinder engine capable of producing 206 bhp. Facing page: (top) the 380SEC; (centre left) the fast 280S; (centre above right) a 1978 350SLC and (centre below right) the 200, for long the basic workhorse of the Mercedes range.

▲ Jaguar Sport XJR-S 6.0

▼ Jaguar Sport XJR 4.0

JAGUAR

'Grace, pace, space'. So ran the most famous Jaguar advertising slogan of all time, and while it is true that the three qualitites have been present in widely varying proportions in the different models, it is also indisputable that they have in most cases been combined in a particularly satisfying way.

Grace, the first of the trilogy, has been embodied in many Jaguars. The SS100 exemplifies the sports cars of the 1930s: a long, louvred bonnet, wire wheels with huge drum brakes, Lucas P100 lamps, cutaway doors, and a rear-mounted spare wheel. For decades afterwards, it inspired copyists, from truly awful Volkswagen-based horrors to the rather lovely Panther J72. Next, the XK-series sports cars exemplified the best styling of the 1950s, though they did get bigger and fatter as they progressed from the XK120 through the XK140 to the XK150; and if you wanted a really graceful saloon, there were the Mk I and Mk II 'baby Jaguars'. In 1961, the E-type took over from the XK150, and seven years later the XJ6 replaced all the other Jaguar saloons. At the time of writing, the last Jaguar to have been introduced was the XJ-S, a startlingly quick motor-car with very individual lines and the most remarkable standards of comfort. There had, however, been rumours of an impending new 'baby Jaguar' saloon for some time. In most cases, pace has been taken for granted. Some of the pre-war saloons may not have been all that fast, at least by modern standards, but the SS100 won races and even sports-car Grands Prix, and all post-war Jaguars with the exception of the pushrod-engined Mk V have been able to top 100 mph, sometimes by 50% or more. In large part, this is due to the 6-cylinder DOHC XK engine, introduced in 1949. It is an astonishingly powerful yet simple unit which has been made in capacities of 2.4, 2.8, 3.4, 3.8 and 4.2 litres (146 ci to 256 ci) with power outputs ranging from 112 bhp (1955 2.4) to 265 bhp (late 4.2 E-types) in road-going form. Since 1971, there has also been a 5.3 litre (323 ci) V-12. In production form it has one cam per bank of cylinders, and propels the manual XJ-S to well over 150 mph; it even hauls the XJ12 saloon (the V12 version of the XJ6) to something approaching the same figure. And these are only the road-going cars: when you consider such legends as the C-type and D-type racers, or the mid-engined 4-cam V12 XJ13, grace and pace were combined to an unbelievable extent, albeit at the expense of space.

Space has in any case always been a more variable commodity. The original SS100 was not a roomy car, and the pre-war saloons were mostly quite modest, but many post-war saloons have been as spacious as anyone could reasonably wish. The 1948 Mk V, the 'Wardour Street Rolls', was big, ostentatious, and no slouch; the 3.5 litre pushrod engine could take it to 91 mph. The Mk VII was a little more rounded than the Mk V, and a little less dignified, but with the XK-series engine it could top 100 mph. The Mk VIII was a Mk VII with detail changes to the body, including a one-piece windscreen, and the Mk IX was a mechanically improved Mk VIII. The ultimate big saloon was the Mk X, later known as the 420, which was nearly seventeen feet long, well over six feet wide, and gave limousine comfort combined with 105 mph performance. The 'baby' Jaguars, introduced in 1955, are generally known generically as the Mk I (before 1959, with the thicker window-frames and roof-pillars) and Mk II, but they are correctly known first by their engine capacities in litres (2.4, 3.4 and 3.8) and then later as the 240 and 340; there was never a 380, though there was a 3.8S. Although very comfortable, and roomy for their overall size, they could not compete with the bigger Jaguar saloons in the space stakes. Since 1968, the XJ6 has of course been the Jaguar for space, and although no one would call it a limousine, its spaciousness is attested by the number that are used by major companies and indeed by the British government as official cars. Lastly, although rear accommodation in the XJ-S is limited, it is a genuine four-seater rather than a 2+2, and the amount of room for the driver and front-seat passenger is as generous as the luxury in which they are cosseted.

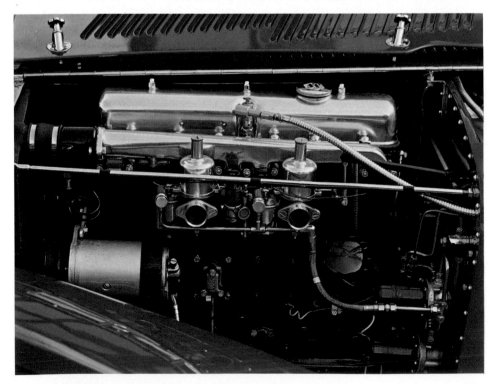

Conventionally styled and outwardly similar to the SS 90, the SS 100 (these pages) was in effect William Lyons' first true production sports car. With its elegant, sweeping lines, excellent handling and lively performance, the car attracted considerable Press interest. In standard road-trim the new car was capable of around 95 mph and a 0-60 time of 12.8 seconds. Not only was the Jaguar a superb performer on the roads, it was soon to prove its worth in international competitions.

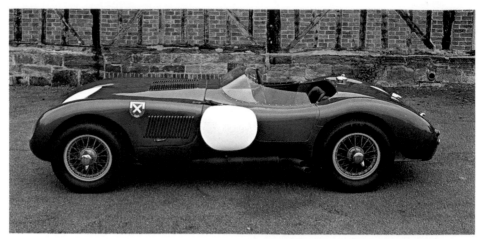

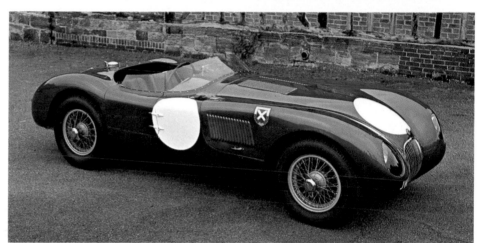

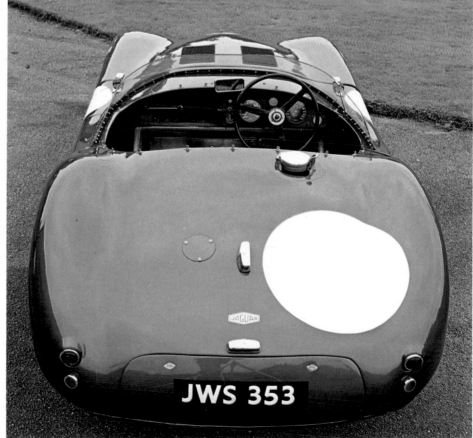

The Mark V (left, far left and above), launched in 1948, was intended as a post-war stop-gap model. It used the old 2.6 and 3.5 litre pushrod engine and a body that was reminiscent of the pre-war cars, but mounted on a new chassis and suspension. A new ohc power unit was being reserved for a totally new Jaguar, which would boast a truly new body shape. The new XK engine, on which the company was pinning its hopes, was first fitted in the XK120 sportscar of 1948. Encouraged by its performance, Jaguar Cars developed a lightweight competition model – the C type. Three cars were entered in the 1951 Le Mans, which resulted in a convincing win for the C type of Whitehead and Walker. Right, above right and top right: a 1952 car from Ecurie Ecosse.

Below: a roadster XK140. Remaining pictures: the legendary XK120, which appeared in 1948 as an open two seater, but later became available in both drophead and fixed head coupé forms. William Lyons is reputed to have designed its classic body shape in less than two weeks. The fixed head variant boasted the more luxurious interior appointments of the saloons; wider doors and a roofline which was fractionally higher than that of the drophead. Although this led to an increase in weight, the FHC suffered little in terms of performance – it was still capable of 120 mph and had a 0-60 time of 9.9 seconds.

The long-awaited Mark VII saloon (these pages), with its race-proved engine, thoroughly tested chassis and torsion bar suspension, and new servo assisted brakes, was launched at the London Motor Show in October 1950. Dressed in its spectacular, flowing bodywork, which had been designed by Lyons and built by the Pressed Steel Company, the car was the sensation of the show and, at a price of under £1,000, was in a class of its own.

After four years of faithful service, the Mark VII was given a face-lift and appeared, in September 1954, as the Mark VII M (these pages). Together with bodywork changes, the engine output was raised from 160 to 190 bhp, and the gearbox ratios were made closer. The alterations resulted in increased top speed and improved fuel consumption.

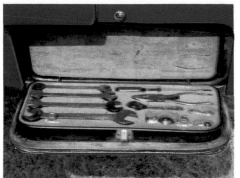

Far left: the XK140 fixed-head coupé was relatively roomy compared to its XK120 predecessor. In 1956 the Mark VII M (bottom and far left inset) was replaced by the short-lived Model VIII (below) which had a one-piece windscreen and minor trim changes together with a new cylinder head which boosted performance.

Largely of monocoque-type construction, the D-type Jaguar (these pages) was a further development of the C-type. The lighter body helped the cars achieve notable victories, including the first four places in the 1957 Le Mans. Later models, such as the yellow vehicle seen here, had a stabilising fin behind the driver.

With the exception of the XJ6, the Mark II, which was available in three engine options, was the company's most successful saloon, both in terms of numbers produced and competition victories. Right, above and top left: a 3.4 litre Mark II from 1963. Far right: the XK150S which, with its 3.8 litre engine, is generally considered the finest car of the XK sports line. Top centre: a white XK150, launched in 1957 and noticeably different from earlier models.

Looking remarkably similar to the D-type, whose monocoque construction it had inherited, the magnificent E-type (these pages) was unveiled at the Geneva Motor Show in 1961. The 3.8 litre engine and gearbox were basically those used in the XK150S, but here was a car with an up-to-the-minute shape that was capable of a staggering 150 mph. Illustrated is a 1962 Series 1 fixed-head coupé.

Far right: the 2.4 litre Mark II was powered by a straight six XK engine, which was designed more for economy than speed. Though it had a top speed of 93 mph, true enthusiasts expected something more and tended to favour the larger engines, particularly the 3.8 which could cut the 2.4's 0-60 time of 17.5 seconds in half. Remaining pictures: an S type of 1963. Powered by either a 3.4 or 3.8 litre engine, the S type was designed to complement the existing Mark II and Mark X.

These pages: the 1966 2+2 E-type, which added a degree of practicality to the car's undoubted panache. Apart from the vehicle's extended wheelbase, the height was increased by 2 inches and the doors were widened considerably to allow access to the rear seats. Mechanical changes on the new car were minimal, but automatic transmission now became an option. A weight increase of 2.5cwt took its toll on performance, but the vehicle could still reach 60 mph in less than 9 seconds.

It is a fitting tribute to the much admired Mark II saloon that well preserved examples can command a higher price today than they did when they left the factory gates. Their incredible smoothness, comfort and fleetness of foot have guaranteed these cars a place in the history of the motor car. The vehicle pictured here is a pristine example of the 1967 2.4 litre Mark II.

Generally considered to be the most significant model ever produced by Jaguar, the XJ6, which appeared in 1968, was to become part of the rationalisation plan that witnessed the gradual demise of all other saloon models. The car had been four years in the making and demand soon far outstripped production. These pages: a 4.2 litre 1972 model that, with the introduction of updated versions, later became known as the Series I.

These pages: the famous lightweight E-type that was raced by the German duo of Peter Lindner and Peter Nocker. Only 12 of these special, aluminium-bodied competition machines were ever built. Powered by a fuel injected 3.8 litre engine which made use of an aluminium block and could deliver 344 bhp, the car was fitted with a five speed ZF gearbox. Top speed of this much modified car, with its aerodynamically designed rear, was in the region of 170mph.

In 1966 the Mark II was put through an economising process which included plastic taking over from leather for the seats. The following year further changes were made and the Mark II disappeared, to be replaced by the 240 and 340 models. The 340 (left and below) was dropped from the range on the appearance of the XJ6, but the 240 (centre left and bottom left) remained. Bottom right and far left: the luxurious 420G which first appeared in 1966 as a replacement for the Mark X, which it greatly resembled.

Originally intended as an option, the 4.2 engine soon became standard on the E-type, as evidenced (below). These pages: the open two-seater, which could be used with its hard top either fitted or removed. Among the Series 2's modifications over its predecessor were: an enlarged air intake, new side/indicator light cluster and the open headlights which had appeared a little earlier. Triple wipers remained for the time being.

Consistent upgrading, production changes and modifications are something that Jaguar have practised on all their ranges, and the XJ saloons have been no exception. In its present form the XJ saloon is available with 3.4 and 4.2 sixes and the 5.3 litre V12. The 2.8 option was dropped in 1973. The long wheelbase variant was introduced in 1972 as the XJ6 L, and has since become standard. Shown here is a Series 3 4.2 litre XJ6 with new-style radiator grille, rear light cluster, door handles, bumpers and wheels.

The XJS was introduced in 1975 as a direct replacement for the E-type. A hard top design was decided on because of legislation which at the time was expected to affect the American market. Though the car's shape met wih a mixed reaction there can be no doubt that the XJS, with performance equal to the E-type and comfort on a par with the saloons, is in the best traditions of the marque. Above, bottom and left: the standard XJS HE and (below) a Lynx Engineering Spyder conversion.

Below: the Lynx Engineering Spyder conversion of the XJS. The high efficiency HE engine, developed in conjunction with an outside team, now features on all the latest 5.3 litre V12 cars (these pages). This Series 3 XJ12 sports re-designed wheel rims and a Jaguar-fitted electric sunroof.

XPG 524Y

FERRARI

In the days before racing cars became travelling billboards, painted in their sponsors' colours and plastered with advertisements, each country had its own racing colours. The British raced in Ulster green, perhaps better known as British Racing Green. French cars were blue, and the Germans used white or silver. Italy's colour was blood red.

Blood red is inseparable from the name of Ferrari. Although the cars have been made in other colours, Italian racing red is for most people synonymous with Ferrari red. The old motto, 'racing improves the breed', has seldom been followed so faithfully as at Modena, and probably no other manufacturer can point to as close an interrelationship between Formula One racers, sports-racers, and production sports cars.

The 'Old Man', Enzo Ferrari, was born in Modena in 1898. Before World War Two, his name was associated mainly with Alfa Romeo, first as competitions manager and then as the head of Scuderia Ferrari, a racing organisation to whom Alfa effectively sub-contracted the business first of winning races, then later of building the cars to win them. After the war, he achieved his lifelong ambition of building a sports-racing car bearing his own name, the Ferrari 125 Competizione. Like so many Ferraris which were to follow, it was powered by a V12 – but a V12 with the astonishingly small capacity of 1.5 litres (91.5 ci). This 'no compromise' approach has been the hallmark of Ferraris ever since.

It would be impossible, except perhaps in an encyclopaedia, to list every Ferrari variation there has been since then. As a small manufacturer with a passionate commitment to racing, sometimes building cars in a 'series' as small as two or three, or even one, the company has remained inseparably associated with V12s, but they have also built in-line fours, V6s, V8s, and flat twelves. The range of capacities has been startling, too, from 1500cc to almost 7 litres (427 ci) with most stops in between. Included angles of the V-engines have been 60°, 65° and 120°, plus of course 180° if you count the flat-twelve as the limiting case of a V12. The engines have been in the front, in the middle, and at the back – although the lattermost layout was used only for racers, when it is a matter of opinion where 'middle' stops and 'back' begins.

It is this bewildering variety which stops Ferrari having the same sort of clearly identifiable image as, say, Porsche. *Everyone* who has ever admired fine cars has heard of Ferrari, and they are almost certain to have seen them racing. But whereas the Porsche 356 was in production for over fifteen years and the 911 was still in production more than twenty years after its introduction, even the best-known Ferraris have been produced in very limited numbers for surprisingly short periods.

Furthermore, the names have been mind-boggling in both variety and complexity. One authority lists over 150 different models, though admittedly many of these are variations on a theme, basically similar cars with different body styles and different states of engine tune. But even where there seems to be a constant thread, there is no way of telling where it leads: 'Dino', in honour of Enzo's son, appears as a part of the name of most or all V6-powered Ferraris, and the old system of numbering the cars according to the capacity of each cylinder is by no means rigidly adhered to. Thus, although the 125C has twelve 125cc cylinders, the 512 is a 5 litre (305 ci) 'twelve' – though a 'B' suffix indicates that it is a 'boxer' or flat motor. To add to the fun, there are suffixes such as GTO ('Gran Turismo Omologato', though it has been suggested that the 'O' was a typing error for which a justification had to be found) and TRS, which stands for 'Testa Rossa Sport'. The 'testa rossa' (red head) in question is not some flame-haired Italian beauty, though: it arose because the cylinder heads of that particular model were once painted red...

Idiosyncratic, exclusive, and blindingly fast, Ferraris have had their ups and downs. As a racing car constructor, Ferrari has done extraordinarily well just to survive for forty years in a business where a single decade can see the birth, zenith, and death of not just one, but several new *marques*. Keeping those cars in the forefront of Formula One competition is even more of an achievement. But to put those race-proved engines into road-going cars is, in the eyes of those who own one of the blood-red cars from Modena, the greatest achievement of all.

Top left: a GTO, much sought after by enthusiasts. Left: the cycle-winged 166 Spyder Corsa. Above: the 330GT 2+2 V12, which was never very popular due to its rather ordinary looks. Below: the 1954 860 Monza, a real brute to drive. Facing page: two views of David Piper's 1965 365P2/3 chassis No. 0836.

Facing page: (top) the mid-engined 250LM, highly successful in competition; (centre) the 1956 410 Superamerica, complete with mid-50s fins; (bottom left) the Type 166 road car of about 1948 with coachwork by Carrozzeria Touring and (bottom right) the V12 275GTB/4, one of the most handsome cars produced by Ferrari. Top left: the 121LM, a not too successful racing car. Top right: a 250GT berlinetta with coachwork by Drogo. Above: a fine 250GTO. Left: a Giovanni Michelotti body on a 1950 195S chassis.

Facing page: (top) a 250GT berlinetta, called the Tour de France, in production from 1955 to 1959; (remaining pictures) the 206SP, perhaps the sleekest and most beautiful Ferrari ever. Top left: the 4.4 litre engine of the Lampredi designed twin overhead camshaft six cylinder 121LM. Above and bottom centre: the elegant 330GTC. Left: the 365GT 2+2. Below: a Dino 246GT. Bottom left and bottom right: one of only three 250LMBs ever built.

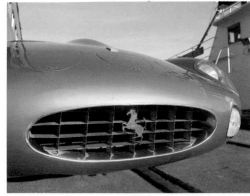

Facing page: two fine 275GTB/4s as restored in America. Top and centre left: a 250GTO, one of a production run of 39. Centre right: a 365GT 2+2. Left: the Dino 246GT, which was relatively inexpensive when it first appeared. Above: a beautiful 1953 340MM, chassis No. 0350, which has been restored to its original two-tone colour scheme by David Cottingham.

Left and below: one of the oldest Ferraris in existence, a 166MM Superleggera Touring Spyder with chassis No. C0161. Owned by former USA race driver Briggs Cunningham, the car now resides in his museum in California. Above: the Rocchi-designed V12 330P4. Above left: a 365 P2/3. Facing page top: a 512M in S specification. The car has been owned and raced by a number of British drivers and is now fully restored to concours condition. Facing page bottom: a 1953 340MM which is stilled raced occasionally.

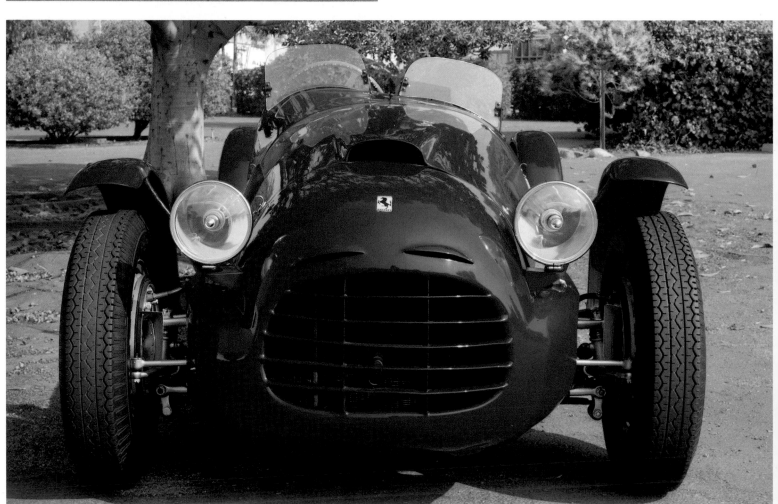

Above: the 750 Monza, whose 4 cylinder 3 litre engine was derived from the 555 engine and whose sleek bodywork was from a design by Ferrari's son Dino. The car was not an overall racing success, being somewhat unpredictable to drive. Top right: the 275 Spyder model. Below: the beautiful V12 275GTB/2, which was in production from 1964 until 1966 when some 460 were produced. Below right and facing page bottom right: the not-too-successful 121LM. Above right, right and facing page top left and top right: the 250GT Spyder California which, unlike the majority of Ferraris which have come from the drawing boards of Pininfarina, was designed by Scaglietti; (centre) the 750 Monza and (bottom left) the 275 Spyder.

Top left and bottom left: a pristine 250GT Spyder. Top centre: an immaculate 365BB whose 12 cylinder boxer engine has a capacity of 4.4 litres and produces 380 bhp at 7,500 rpm. Top: the seating arrangements of the luxurious 365GTB4, more commonly known as the Daytona. It had a long production run of some 1,300 vehicles turned out between 1968 and 1973 and is one of the legendary Ferraris. Above: the cover for the rear-mounted transverse engine of the 308GTB. Left: the 250GT Spyder California. Above left: the 246GT in the early days was not exactly a well put-together car, but by dint of hard work on the part of their owners most models around today are of concours standard.

Facing page and below: the 206SP, whose ancestry can be dated back to Vittorio Jano's design of the 65 degree four cam V6 F2 of 1956. Top: the 246GT, whose V6 2.4 litre engine was produced in the FIAT factory. Above and left: the model called the Modulo. This was undoubtedly the wildest design ever executed on a Ferrari chassis. Though impractical for road use, the car shows the genius of the Pininfarina designers.

Facing page: (centre left) the 308 Spyder, with the detachable roof in place; (top, centre right and bottom left) the 308GT4 2+2, which appeared in 1973 and (bottom right) the Ferrari Penin, the first four door saloon to bear the Ferrari name. Left, bottom left and bottom right: the front-engined 4.4 litre V12 365GTB/4 which was in production for five years, beginning in 1968. Below left: a front view of the 512BB, giving an impression of brute strength. Below: a 308 whose front spoiler adds to the overall flowing symmetry of the car.

Left: the smooth, flowing lines of the 308GTBi. Bottom: the low-slung, racy outline of the 308GTSi. Below and facing page: the 512BBi, which was called by some the flagship of the Ferrari fleet and by others Ferrari's Macho Missile. The 12 cylinder horizontally opposed engine has a capacity of 4,943cc and lies longitudinally behind the driver. The 512BBi is hardly in keeping with grand touring, as the amount of space available for luggage is minimal.

CADILLAC

It is hard to choose the ultimate Cadillac. The company has, after all, been in business since 1902, and has manufactured everything from a 1.6 litre (98.2 ci) single-cylinder runabout to a series of V16s, via in-line fours, V8s, and V12s.

For sheer magnificence, the V16s are hard to beat. Introduced in December 1929 with a 7406 cc (452 ci) displacement, a number were sold with roadster bodies which look rather odd to European eyes – two seats and a huge trunk which concealed a dickey, or 'rumble seat' – and such delightful excesses as not two, but three beautifully finished external hinges for the rearward-opening doors, and matching trunks which really were trunks, complete with trunk-handles and fastening clips to hold them to the luggage rack. The big sedan bodies were cathedral-like in their dignity (and size!), and the dual-cowl phaetons were as elegant as anything on the road. Unlike many European super-luxury cars, most Cadillacs were sold with factory bodies, rather than as bare chassis.

Few manufacturers have offered a V12 as a second string – few enough have offered them as a flagship – but that is exactly what Cadillac did with the Series 370, introduced at 6030 cc (368 ci) in 1931; the V8 layout, introduced in 1915 and still in use today for the flagship models, was the 'cooking' engine from 1929 to 1940, when the V16 finally died. The V12s are often every bit as attractive as the V16s, which is also what the buyers thought at the time; they cut deeply into the sales of the bigger car in the depression years.

The original 1915 V8 was very much a car of its time, apart from the extremely impressive engine, which was the first mass-produced V8. Thereafter, between-wars V8 styling was very variable indeed, with the best-looking cars the equal of any, anywhere, and the worst as ordinary as any 'grey porridge'. Surprisingly, a number of very good-looking Cadillacs were not Cadillacs at all: they were La Salles, introduced in 1927 as a lower-cost extension to the Cadillac line and phased out in 1940.

After the war, Cadillac standardised on the V8 (which eventually grew to 500 ci, 8.2 litres) and let the stylists have a free hand. The late 1940s and early 1950s saw the kind of styling which now epitomises the period, with the Coupe de Ville almost foreshadowing the 'low riders' of two and three decades later, but as the 1950s progressed, the hand of the stylist became more and more obvious. As early as 1955 there were overtones of the bullet (or breast) motif which was to reach its peak in 1959, and more than a hint of the fins which would become unbelievable in the same year. From 1955 to 1959 the breast-and-fin approach became more and more exaggerated, until it finally degenerated into parody; looking at the 1959 Eldorado Biarritz, one is tempted to ask if 'Biarritz' was actually a typing error for 'bizarre'. After that high-point, styling gradually became more conservative again, until by the end of the 1960s and through most of the 1970s Cadillacs were big, well-executed, and really rather ordinary.

There was something of a resurgence in styling, though this time in rather better taste, in the late 1970s and early 1980s with the handsome Seville, though sadly the junior stylists were again unable to resist over-egging the pudding, the quilted padding and other excesses crept in by the mid-1980s. Then there was the Cimarron, a small, four-cylinder, front-wheel-drive car which excited as much antagonism from Cadillac purists as the 924 did from Porsche purists, but it is (one hopes) merely a passing fad; it is a pleasant little car, but it is not a Cadillac.

Despite their impressive size, Cadillacs have always been designed to be easy to drive. They adopted electric starting in 1912, and they took up Oldsmobile's HydraMatic transmission only a year after Oldsmobile brought it out in 1940. That they have always been luxurious is also beyond dispute, although it is really only the pre-war cars which invite comparison with firms like Rolls-Royce, Daimler, Isotta-Fraschini, Delage and Delahaye. Since then, American luxury has headed in the direction of ostentation, while European luxury has generally tended towards understatement, though there have been exeptions such as Monteverdi and arguably Lagonda. Even so, the observation which was made at the beginning still holds: it is hard to choose the ultimate Cadillac. In a way, there is a lot to be said for the Biarritz...

▲ 1989 Cadillac 60 Special

▼ 1989 Cadillac Allante

Left: the 1903 Cadillac Model A runabout. This model had a single cylinder of 98.2 cubic inch displacement, but its 9¾ horsepower gave it a top speed of 30 mph. Above and top: the absence of doors and the pronounced rake of the windscreen give the 1910 Cadillac Roadster a decidedly sporting air. With its four separately cast cylinders the car could manage more than 50 mph.

With its streamline cowl, electric lights and left-hand steering – all found on 1914 Cadillacs – the underhood revolution on this 1915 Model-15 touring car isn't apparent. This was the first year of the 90-degree V8 L-head engine, a layout destined to dominate Cadillac thinking for over 30 years.

This 1924 V-63 five passenger coupé has a body by Fisher. Incorporated in the closed body refinements are a ventilating windshield, a big sun visor and some trunk space. As yet front bumpers were not standard, though this vehicle has the optional spare rim and tyre. Beneath the surface lies the smoothness of the 90-degree crankshaft and the stopping power of the marque's first four-wheel brakes.

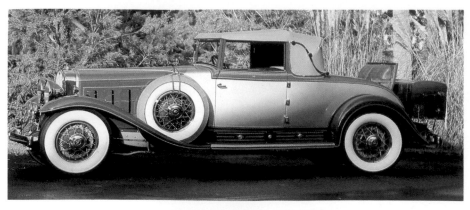

These pages: the ultimate in V16s. A 1930 Model-452 Fleetwood two-passenger convertible coupé with the Madam-X type slightly slanted vee-windshield, and the sweep-panel two-toning pioneered by LeBaron's Ralph Roberts. All the 'Classic' equipment is present – six wire wheels, dual sidemounts in canvas covers, twin spot lamps, dual trumpet horns and a big rear trunk.

These pages: a Series 345 LaSalle Fleetwood roadster of 1930. Maybe it's too close to a Cadillac with 340 cubic inches of V8 under the bonnet against the senior make's 355, an output only slightly inferior, and a wheelbase just six inches shorter. Visible are the cowl louvres which distinguish Fleetwood coachwork from the cheaper Fishers.

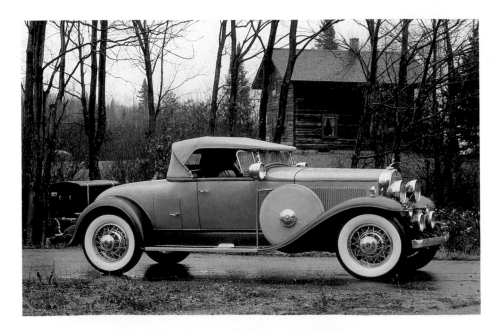

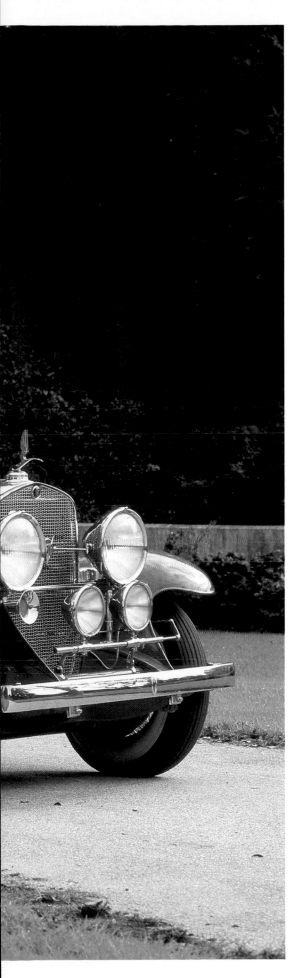

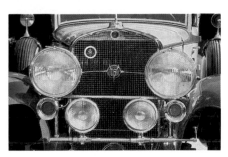

In 1932 the V16 went into its second season unchanged as the Series 452-A. This one is a slant-windshield Fleetwood convertible coupé in GM's regulation ragtop idiom of the time. On an advertised 165 hp, the V16 would attain 100 mph, though the absence of audible power was enough attraction for most customers.

Right: a Series 345 LaSalle Fleetwood roadster of 1930. Below and bottom right: a 1931 eight-cylinder, dual-cowl phaeton, which came complete with all the usual extras: twin spot lamps, hood louvres, a Goddess mascot and the whitewall tyres usually reserved for formal town vehicles. Bottom left: a 1930 452 V16 complete with the rare wooden wheels and demountable rims. Far right: a 1931 452-A by Fleetwood.

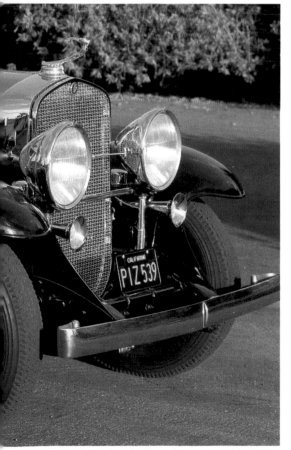

The American custom body era was over by 1940. This vehicle is one of only three long-chassis Model-75 V8s of the 1940 model run supplied to custom coachbuilders, in this case Brunn of Buffalo. The cowl is stock Cadillac, but the rest is true custom.

Below centre: the vast 1947 Model-75 on the 136-inch wheelbase has been modified by Derham into a formal sedan by the deletion of the rear quarterlights and the addition of landau irons and a fabric top. Remaining pictures: the 1947 Model-62 convertible, which is little different from the 1942 version.

Sixty Special influences have rubbed off on this 1941 6267D convertible coupé. The rear fender skirts are optional, the fenders, lamps and grille are not integrated and there's not much left of the running boards. The mascot has been stylised and the left hand tail lamp conceals the gas cap.

The 1955 Model-62 convertible (these pages) is an enormous car, measuring 216 inches long and 80 inches wide. The grille is still unmistakably Cadillac, however, and the ponderous dummy air intakes of the early '50s have faded into a minor outburst in vertical chromium. The latest 331 cubic inch V8 pushed out 250 horsepower on a 9:1 compression ratio.

At the top of the post-war range was this Fleetwood 75. If the regular Cadillac seemed big, this one's vital statistics were formidable: a wheelbase of nearly 150 inches, a bumper-to-bumper length of 236 inches and a weight of som 5,000 pounds. Four cigar lighters, two electric clocks and power brakes, seats and windows and divider were part of this 1956 package, while air conditioning was an established regular option. Demand for such a vehicle was, of course, limited but sales stayed around a steady 1,500 per year throughout the decade.

The supercar of 1957 was the Eldorado Brougham, with air suspension, which cost $13,074, compared with $6,648 for the exotic Eldorado Biarritz convertible and $4,713 for a 62 sedan. Styling was four-door pillarless hardtop with a brushed stainless steel roof, which shows up well in these pictures. Detail was most elaborate, as witness the big glovebox, which came complete with six magnetised tumblers and a cigarette case, on the facia (left) and the smoker's companion (centre left). Note also the growth of the tail fins.

The outrageous tail fin and rear light treatment was reaching its ultimate in the 1959 Eldorado Biarritz convertible. The 390 cubic inch valve-in-head V8 managed to put out 345 horsepower thanks to triple two-barrel carburettors. Quad headlamps were standard by now, as were nearly all extras other than air conditioning. Convertibles were still good business, too: Cadillac sold 1,320 of this model, despite its $7,400 price tag. The Eldorado script aft of the front wheel arch was a quick recognition feature.

The easiest way to tell the cheaper 62 convertible from the Biarritz is the full length rubbing strip. The 62 had only a single quadrajet carburettor on its 390 cubic inch engine and power output was down slightly to 320 horsepower. Above and top: the Coupé de Ville and (right) the Sedan de Ville versions of the 62, which both featured a 130 inch wheelbase and optional power assistance for pretty well everything. The huge, sweeping fins were matched by an equally aggressive grille and there was also a mini-grille at the rear.

In 1968, Cadillac's de Ville convertible still used a conventional rear-wheel drive chassis of 129½ inch wheelbase, though this dimension was just about the only one that wasn't on the up. Between '67 and '68 the cars acquired an extra 6½ inches of hood, while piston displacement rose from 429 to 472 cubic inches. Integration was carried a step further by parking the windshield wipers out of sight, where they sometimes stayed thanks to snow and autumn leaves. Convertible production stayed steady at around 18,000 units a year.

The 1967 new generation Eldorado Fleetwood hardtop came a year behind the Olds Toronado and was built on similar principles. Oldsmobile, however, did not include such refinements as variable ratio power steering and automatic level control. Though the new Cadillac shared its body with the Olds and Buick's Riviera, it was still every inch a Cadillac. An impressive hood meant more than compact dimensions, so a short wheelbase did not make for a much smaller car.

Right: one of just 200 'limited edition' Eldorado convertibles produced in 1966 which were thought to mark the end of the ragtop era. Inset top right: the 1977 Fleetwood Eldorado, one of the last truly large Cadillacs. Below and bottom: a 1979 Seville which, when it appeared in 1975, marked a return to compact proportions with a wheelbase of 114 inches. Below centre: the 1971 second generation Eldorado, which was destined to be the basis for all Cadillac's remaining convertibles. A massive look is imparted by the energy-absorbing bumpers and the coffin-nose hood on this 222-inch-long model.

A 1980 Cadillac Seville Elegante sedan in two-tone metallic silver. The model features front wheel drive and all-disc brakes, with a choice of either a 368 cubic inch gasoline or 350 cubic inch diesel V8 motor. Engineering rationalisation at GM threatened Cadillac's individuality, but the bustle-back, razor-edge sedan body was peculiar to the Seville.

▲ Rolls-Royce Silver Spur II

▼ Rolls-Royce Corniche III

ROLLS ROYCE

'The best car in the world' resulted from the unlikely partnership of a perfectionist practical engineer from the Midlands, and the daredevil third son of Lord Llangattock. The Honourable Charles Stewart Rolls, automobilist, racing driver and aviator, was impressed with the motor-cars designed by Frederick Henry Royce: in December 1904, the two men agreed to hyphenate their surnames as a trade-mark, and in March 1906 Rolls-Royce Ltd was registered as a company.

Since then, the Rolls-Royce has become as much a legend as a means of transport. The famous Silver Ghost, with its aluminium-finished coachwork and silver-plated brightwork; the 'baby' Rolls-Royce Twenty; the mighty Phantoms; the 20/25; the Wraith, and its post-war successor the Silver Wraith, the Silver Dawn, the first Rolls-Royce to be supplied with a standard body, instead of in chassis form; the Silver Cloud; the Silver Shadow; the Corniche; the Camargue; and the Silver Spur. Even the engines are legendary: the great straight-sixes of seven litres-plus (over 427 ci), the V12 of the 1936 Phantom III, and the current V8 with its rated horse-power of 'sufficient'.

There are as many apocryphal stories as true ones about the Rolls-Royce, but some of the true ones are stranger than the apocrypha. For example, the original Silver Ghost really did run from London to Edinburgh using only top gear in 1911, and the famous 15,000 mile reliability run really did take place in 1907, in the same car; the total cost of parts to restore it to as-new specification afterwards was £2 2s 7d (£2.13 in modern money, or about $10 at the exchange rate in 1907). Again, the Phantom IV really is only available to special order for royalty and heads of state, and its engine is a massive straight-eight used in no other car. The Phantom V and VI (the current model) have the standard V8.

On the other hand, there is no truth in the rumour that Rolls-Royce maintain large, covered vans in which dirty Rolls-Royces are spirited away to be washed, regardless of their owners' wishes; and the enduring story of the man who telephoned about the bill for an axle failure which had been repaired the previous year, only to be told, 'Rolls-Royces do not break axles', has so far proved impossible to authenticate. But there really is a special school for chauffeurs whose employers require them to drive Rolls-Royces, and Indian Maharajahs really did order their cars to the most extraordinary specifications – everything finished in gold and ivory, for example, or equipped with gun-racks and searchlights for tiger shooting at night. Their modern equivalents, the oil sheikhs, really do use Rolls-Royces for beach buggies. Devotees of Sri Bhagwan Rajneesh, the guru who founded the 'Orange People', really did give him more than three dozen Rolls-Royces.

Apart from the first few heady years, when Rolls entered Royces and then Rolls-Royces in races and time trials – and indeed won the 1906 TT – these magnificent cars have always been slightly old-fashioned, but for the very best of reasons. The Honourable Charles Stewart Rolls was killed in a flying accident in 1910, and without his flamboyant partner to egg him on, Frederick Henry Royce gave his conservatism full rein. He was determined never to adopt any mechanical feature until it was thoroughly proven. Once he had satisfied himself of its worth, he would adopt it, even if it meant paying royalties to another manufacturer. Hispano-Suiza contributed servo brakes on pre-war cars; the modern automatic gearbox is based on the General Motors HydraMatic unit; and the self-levelling suspension of the Shadow owes more than a little to Citroen.

What is it, though, that makes these cars such a legend? A cynic would reply that it was the price: charge enough for anything, and you will find a fool to buy it. A snob would say that it was because it was the *only* car in which to be seen. A self-made man might say that it showed that he had 'arrived'. A lover of fine engineering would point to the sheer quality of the machinery; a lover of luxury could point to the finish and furnishings. But all of these are only partial answers. A Rolls-Royce is more than the sum of its parts. Most people only ever ride in a Rolls-Royce at a wedding or at a funeral; but the people who own them almost always give the same answer when you ask them why they bought one. With an understatement which is almost as impressive as the vehicle itself, they reply, 'Because it's a good car'.

Facing page: (top) the original Silver Ghost and a modern Camargue coupé styled by Pininfarina of Turin and (bottom) a 1912 Hooper Limousine on the 40/50 chassis, with the high roof and vertical windscreen of the period. Top: a 1912 vehicle with a Roi de Belges body, popularised by the King of the Belgians, who was interested in motor sports, on the 40/50 Silver Ghost chassis. Above: the 1904, ten horsepower twin-cylinder car. Left: a high and handsome cabriolet on the 1911 Ghost chassis.

Below, above right and facing page top: the company's own Silver Ghost. With its aluminium-painted body and silver-plated accessories, this Barker-bodied open tourer became the inspiration for the name which is now applied to all examples of the model. Below right: a 1916 landaulette body on a Silver Ghost chassis. The tubular front bumper and cylindrical headlamps suggest an American origin. Bottom: a handsome 20 Tourer of 1926 with a body by Barker, official works coachbuilders of the time. Facing page bottom: an unusual 1911 limousine body by Lawton of Liverpool with a tulip back and six running lamps. Above: a 1931 Phantom Two Continental.

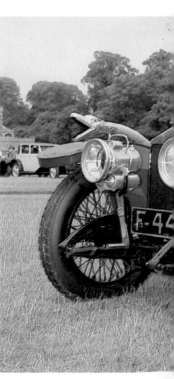

Top left: a typical Ghost tourer. Left: a 1913 Ghost with a body built by the Indian firm of Khan. Above: a modern, jury-rigged ignition coil keeps this 1912 Ghost engine running. Right: a 1918 40/50 Ghost with an Auster rear screen. Below right: an American Silver Ghost built at the Springfield factory in 1922. Below: a 1911 Silver Ghost with the low bonnet line in the sporting manner. Far left: a 1913 Ghost with a limousine body.

Facing page: (top) a 1929 two-ton tourer Phantom, which replaced the Ghost but was still known as the 40/50, and (bottom) an American car with the distinctive indented wheelnuts, white-wall tyres and cylindrical lamps. Above: a fine, Barker-bodied tourer from 1925, the last year of Silver Ghost production. Left: a sporting Ghost with a light, skiff-type body in two-seater form. This is the 1912 twin-carburettor version, based on the Alpine Eagle or Continental model. Below: a 1914 Ghost, described as a Colonial model, with Auster rear screen, rear luggage rack and both handbrake and gear-change mounted outside the bodywork.

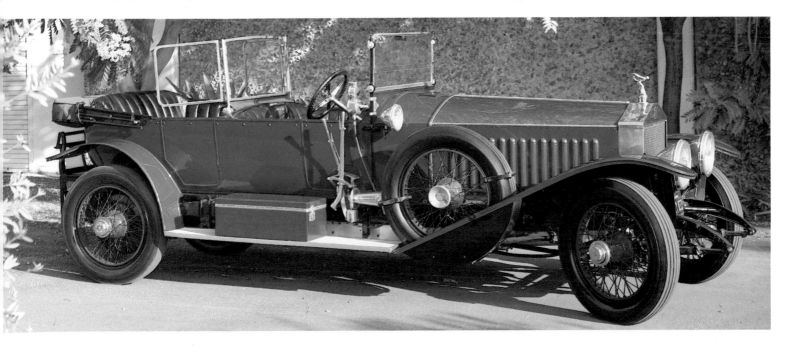

Below and right: a 1923 Twenty. Below centre: a 1926 Twenty with a later Compton body. Bottom: a typical 1930s drophead coupé. Facing page: (top left) a 1912 Hooper Limousine on the Ghost chassis; (top right) an Alpine Eagle Silver Ghost; (centre right) a 1925 Twenty with a Barker 'doctor's coupé' body and (bottom) a 1910 Silver Ghost open tourer by Barker. Overleaf: a Phantom I tourer made for the the Nawab of Hyderabad.

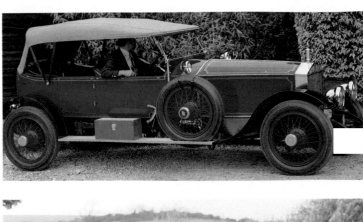

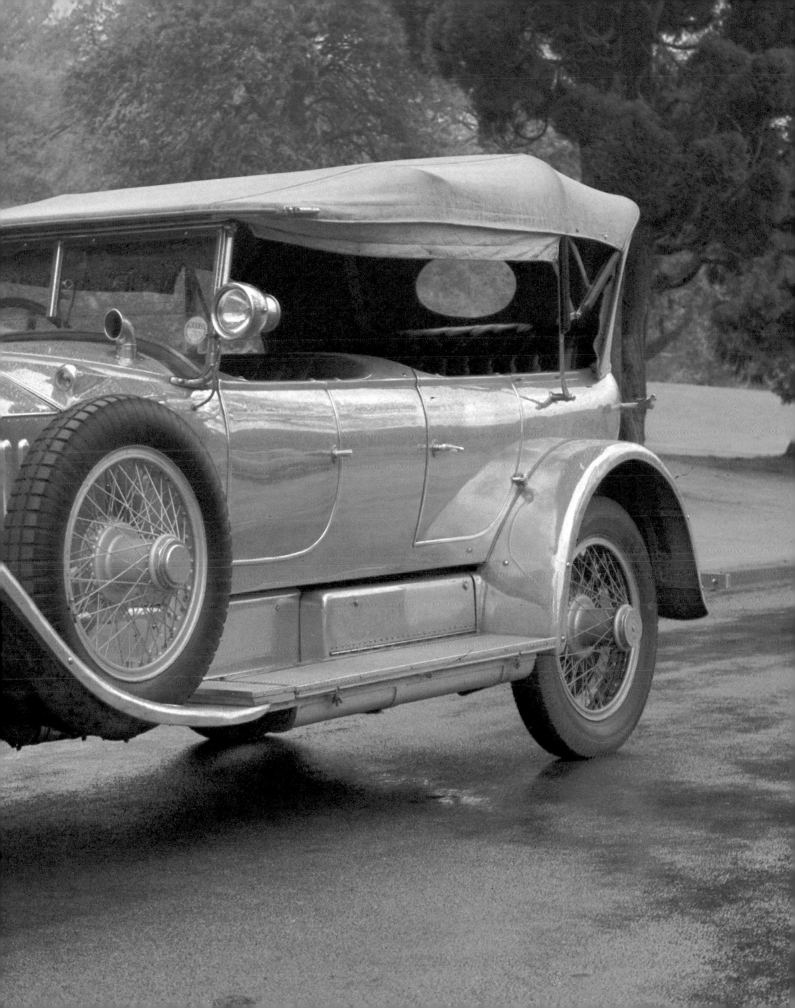

Facing page: (top) a 1923 Barker-bodied tourer on the Twenty chassis with a splendid bulb-horn on the offside running board and (bottom) a 1914 Silver Ghost four-seat tourer. The sporting wind-screen, built-out wire wheels and herringbone-pattern tyres give an authentic air. Left: an imposing Phantom I in sedanca form. The Phantom I had the advantages of front brakes, helped by a servo-system, and a detachable head on its six cylinders. Below: a 1934 Phantom II sedanca. Bottom: a Twenty four-seat tourer with rear Auster screen and rear half-tonneau.

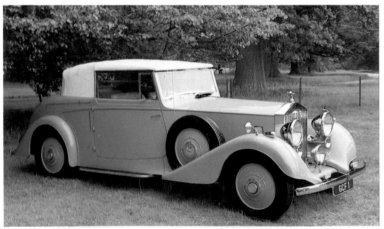

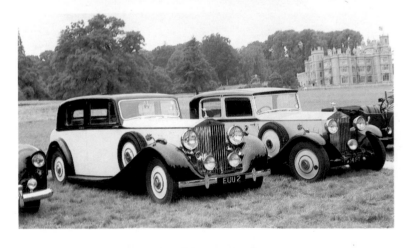

Left: a 1928 Phantom I saloon. Above: an Anglo-American Phantom II of 1929 with a body originally built by Park Ward, but reworked by Brewster in 1932. Right: a sporting Phantom. Below right: a three-door coupé Phantom I. Bottom right: a 1911 Silver Ghost limousine. Below: a barrel-sided tourer with bodywork by Barker. Bottom left: a 1938 Hooper-bodied Phantom III, licence plate EUU 2, with formal, four-door saloon coachwork beside an earlier Phantom. Below left: a drophead coupé body built on a 25/30 chassis by the Belgian coach-builder Vanden Plas.

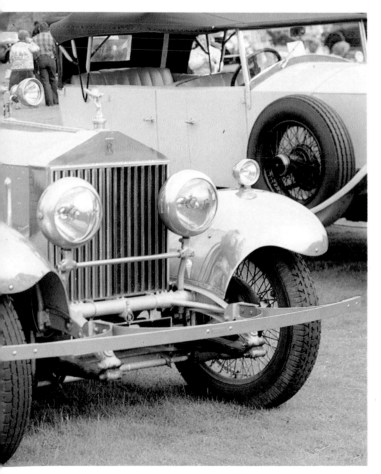

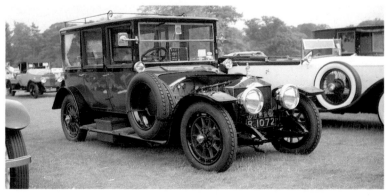

Top: a Silver Ghost tourer with
sidewings to the windscreen
and an Auster screen. Facing
page top: a 1927 Phantom I
with Sedanca-de-ville bodywork. Facing page bottom: a
1913 Ghost with cantilever
springs. Right: a four-door, four-
light Wraith saloon of 1938.
Above: a Thrupp & Maberly
sedanca body on a Phantom II
chassis with individual running
boards, or steps. Above right: a
handsome Phantom II drop-
head coupé bodied by H.J.
Mulliner with wheel discs and
unusual body colour.

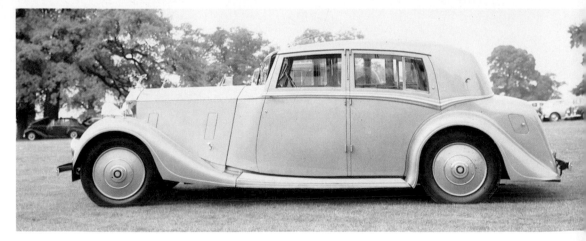

Above: a 1930 Thrupp & Maberly sports cabriolet de ville Phantom II. Right and facing page bottom: Bentley, who were bought out by Rolls-Royce on their collapse in 1933, made this magnificent 6.5 litre sports car in 1930 and then ran out of money. Rolls-Royce feared these cars as competitors and bought the company to keep it out of competitors' hands. The vintage Bentleys, as opposed to the Derby Bentleys built by Rolls, are now much sought after by enthusiasts. Below: a Springfield Phantom with Brewster body and American bumpers, white sidewall tyres, Brookes rear trunk, American headlamps and cantilever springs. Facing page top: a rebodied 1926 Twenty which was fitted with this foursome drophead coupé body in the '30s style.

Above and left: the three-litre Bentley speed model produced before the takeover by Rolls-Royce. Top right: the exceptionally elegant 1933 Phantom II Continental faux-cabriolet with twin rear-mounted spare wheels. Right: an American-registered Phantom III of 1936 with unusual rear-wheel spats, shallow windscreen and whitewall tyres. Bottom right: a 1938 Phantom III with a formal Hooper limousine body with division between driver and passengers. Below: the 1952 R-Type Continental Bentley, powered by a straight six engine.

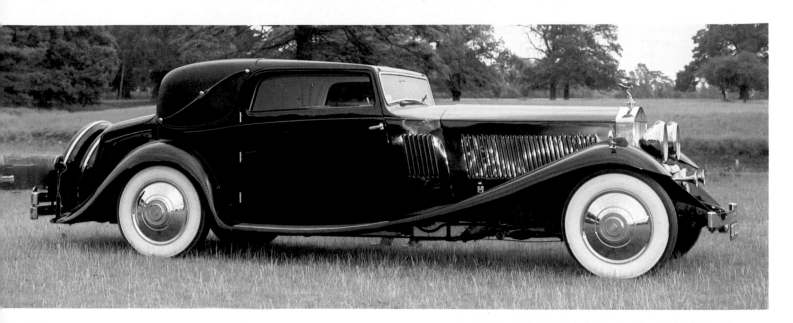

Facing page: the imposing front of a 1930s drophead coupé with four seat body and the usual impressive display of horns, driving lights and headlamps. Left: the Phantom VI, the largest of the current Rolls-Royce models, is powered by the 6,750cc V8 engine that was originally developed for the Silver Shadow II. Below: a 1931 sedanca-de-ville on the 20/25 chassis. Bottom left: a Phantom III. Bottom right: an elegant body on a Phantom, with twin side-mounts in metal holders and a collection of horns and lights on the front apron.

Top left: a Wraith produced in 1939, the year in which Rolls-Royce bought out Park Ward. Top right: a 20/25 sports saloon with body by Barker. The 20/25 was a development of the Twenty and was made between 1929 and 1936. Above and right: a sedanca-de-ville body by the French coachbuilders Fenandez and Darrin on a 20/25 chassis. Above right: a 1936 20/25 cabriolet by Offord. Facing page: (top) a four-door, six-light saloon on the 20/25 chassis; (centre left) a Silver Wraith of 1949; (centre right) a 1934 20/25 with bodywork by Connaught, and (bottom) a 1949, Hooper-bodied Silver Wraith, the company's first post-war car.

Facing page: a 1982 Silver Spur, a long wheel-base version of the Silver Spirit. Above: the Phantom VI, the most exclusive motor car in the world, with hand-built bodywork by Mulliner Park Ward. This seven-seater is 19ft 10in long and includes television, telephone, radio and cocktail cabinet. Left and below: two examples of the magnificent, sporting-style Corniche convertible. Overleaf: possibly the ultimate motor car, the Bentley Mulsanne Turbo.

Facing page: (top) the massive Phantom VI which, since 1979, has been powered by the V8 unit used in other models and (bottom) a Bentley Mulsanne with American model headlights. Left: the Silver Spirit. It is fitted with automatic air-conditioning and automatic gearbox as standard. The 6,750cc V8 engine is run for the equivalent of 50 miles on natural gas on the test bed. Twelve coats of paint are applied for the perfect body finish. Below left: the elegant Corniche convertible with a hand-built, two-door body by Mulliner Park Ward. Below: a Silver Shadow II, introduced in 1977. Bottom: the Camargue, designed by Pininfarina and produced in limited numbers, had bodywork by Mulliner Park Ward.

Facing page: the Corniche convertible and (inset) the two-door Camargue. Top: the Bentley version of the two-door, fixed head Corniche coupé. Above: the elegant Corniche convertible, the first model to appear with the larger 6,750cc V8 engine and improved air conditioning. Left: the long-wheelbase Silver Wraith Mark II. Overleaf: (bottom left) a two-door Camargue and (top left and right) the Silver Spirit.

Acknowledgement

The publishers wish to acknowledge the assistance provided by the following in the compilation of this book:

A G Hendry
A W Smith
Alan Hanes
Alan Hodges
Alan Minchin
Andrew Bell
Auburn Cord-Duesenberg Museum
Autocar Magazine
B R Cracknell
Ben Caskey and family
Bill Arnold
Bill Lake
Bob Edson
Brian Wagstaff
C W Hughes
Charles Coleman and 'Toni'
Curt Marketti
D Birch
David Cottingham

Delbert Fellers
Denis Winebrenner
Don Andrews
Don Ayres
Don Peterson
Dorothy and Jerry Coburn
Dr Ing h c Porsche AG
Edward Eves
Elliott Museum
Ferrari Owners' Club
Ferrari, Modena, Italy
Fred De Vault
Gary and Lori Shuman
Geoff Brooks
George Bishop
Gerald Paradise
Godfrey Eaton
Gordon Clark
Guy Salmon Ltd
Hadzera Wright
Harold Meyer
Jaguar Cars
Jim Ringberg
John Blake

John Nichols
Keith Bluemel
L Harper
Larry Riesen
Les Eveson
Lindsey Goodman
Maranello Concessionaires Ltd
Melvyn Fancy
Michael Cotton
Michael Sedgwick
Mike Butler
Mike Hayes
Mike Triboulet
Nelson Bandy
Nicky Wright
Paul Cizek
Paula Kash
Pete Kesling
Peter and Dulce Lawson
Peter Hall
Peter McCabe
Philip Speer

Picture Library Porsche
Porsche Cars Great Britain Ltd
Presseabteilung Daimler-Benz AG
Richard Carpenter
Richard Embling
Rick Carroll
Robert Rodgers
Rolls-Royce Motors Ltd
Ron Buch
Ron Lintz
Roy Bleeke
Sanderson's Auto Sales
Skip and Cathy Marketti
Steven R. Keusch
Stratford Motor Museum
The Elliott Museum
The Randinelli Family
The Riekes
Tom Lester
Tom Walker
Van Hallan – Photo-Features
Vernon Crews
Will Athawes
William Clark
Willy Khan